why water
just won't do

Wine Matters

why water just won't do

Malcolm Gluck

with illustrations by Mark McCrum

Little Books by Big Names™

To Araucaria, the wily old tease

First published in the United Kingdom in 2003 by Little Books Ltd,
48 Catherine Place, London SW1E 6HL

10 9 8 7 6 5 4 3 2 1

A CIP catalogue record for this book is available from the British Library.

ISBN: 1 904435 04 1

*Many thanks to: Mark McCrum for illustrations, Jamie Ambrose for editorial
management, Ghost for original jacket styling, jacket photographs and
illustration, Mousemat Design for jacket and text design, Margaret Campbell
of Scan-Hi Digital and Craig Campbell of QSP Print for printing consultancy,
and Ann Barrett for indexing. Printed and bound in Scotland by Scotprint.*

contents

You should approach each new bottle of wine as you would a new acquaintance: hoping to be elevated and intrigued, but above all, hoping that friendship develops.

<small>CENNUS</small>

<small>(TRANSLATED BY BENITO VARGA)</small>

introduction

Wine is a fermented product, but this titchy tome is a distillation. In other words, I have tried to concentrate within these pages much of the most useful information, short of recommending actual bottles and providing a vineyard guide, that the modern wine-drinker will find of general value.

This is not a book that I hope only the newcomer to wine will find fascinating – although it is true to say that the debutante will find a wealth of revelation within. For the more experienced drinker, too, there is a good deal to capture the imagination, to inform the mind, and to strengthen the delights of the subject.

This is a simple, straightforward book broken down into five sections. The first deals with the current situation concerning health. Wine is now widely seen by science and medicine as a 'health drink', if I may so term it without trying to be cute. As part of an intelligent diet, wine-drinking within the drinker's capacity and comfort is now recognized as a positive attribute of living.

The second section covers – of necessity, briefly yet (I hope) cogently – the techniques involved in matching wine with food. This is an important area, much misunderstood by many so-called experts, upon which I hope I can shed light and offer some practical elucidations. Many old wives' tales are demolished (such as fish must be eaten with dry white wine), and new ideas on food-and-wine matching are offered.

Section three is devoted to various and sundry wine 'rules' – more specifically, why so many of them don't matter a jot when it comes to enjoying wine. The first part of this section, extremely topically, deals with the current debate about why the cork seal in a wine is now outdated and why alternative closures are being employed more and more. There is much here that is new or not much discussed, and I hope I can both give the reader some insight and offer some really useful advice and pointers to the future.

The remainder of section three deals with the thorny subjects of wine experts (should you believe them or not), price (does higher really mean better quality), and – that French textbook favourite – *terroir* (what it is and why it really doesn't matter as much as the aforementioned 'experts' would have you believe). All of which is an attempt to give you the confidence to trust your own judgements, and value your own palate. It asks, and hopefully answers, some of the fundamental questions to do with wine appreciation. It is an exposure of some of the problems faced by wine-drinkers, and what I see as the solutions.

The fourth section takes this one step further and examines how the changing attitudes towards European (by which I mean mainly French) 'traditions' that surround wine have caused modern wine-drinkers at last to vote with their palates and move their thirsts elsewhere. This state of affairs is quite exciting for wine-lovers throughout the world, but not, of course, for France itself, which, if it cannot move with the times, will become left behind.

The last and fifth section is concerned with wines you should know about for all the right reasons. Not because they are famous or expensive, but because they are affordable and worth getting to know. Now I stress that these are not individual bottles; I am providing here a guide to areas worth seeking out, and vineyard names worth keeping up your sleeve.

In essence (which is what a distillation is), this is a book to enjoy as a concentrated introduction to the latest thinking on the most awesome, delicious, complex, rewarding liquid on the planet.

1

why wine matters
to health

Here I am keen to suggest that wine is a
health drink for well-founded reasons.
Wise wine-drinkers live longer and
are healthier than teetotallers.
Wine is a great Gift of Nature.

Alcohol is an emotive issue. Fortunately, in this country, it is a liquid objected to only by a minority, from the devoutly religious to the misinformed and cranky. According to one way of thinking, alcohol cannot possibly be good for you since it is not naturally occurring in Nature; therefore it is a devilish aberration of Humankind.

In response to this, I would say firstly that alcohol is obviously (and tragically) to be avoided by those who are allergic to it, and this includes those who are predisposed to become alcohol-dependent. But then the same has to be said about certain individuals and nuts (I refer to the hard-shelled fruits of certain trees and shrubs here, not the persons espousing these views). Who, in full and sane possession of his or her faculties, would ban peanuts on the grounds that 0.0005 percent of the population has zero tolerance to them?

There is also the notion of what it is that constitutes intelligent or moderate drinking. I do not say that drinking three bottles of wine in a single day will do you more good than harm, for indeed this level of quaffing is dangerous. It leads to severe dehydration and body-organ overload. But three bottles spread evenly over a week? With, perhaps, food? All part of a modest and healthy diet for a healthy drinker.

This leaves the canard that alcohol – or, to put it more scientifically, the fermentation process by which chemical changes in certain fruits or vegetables convert sugars and starches from one thing into another – is a devious invention of the human mind. Not entirely so. Fermentation occurs in Nature, naturally. The yeasts and enzymes that create the ferment which leads to alcohol are not only present in many of Nature's products (including bread) but also in the human gut.

Alcohol is a word derived from the Arabic *al-kohl* or *al-kuhl*, a cosmetic substance created via distillation which, centuries ago, was used as eye make-up. The distillation process was invented in the Middle East, mainly to create perfumes – highly aromatic and alcoholic spirits – from flowers and plants.

Wine is made by a different process. It is the conversion, by fermentation, of sugar into alcohol from fruit. Grapes are unusually rich in the chemicals necessary to achieve a degree of alcohol unmatched by any other fruit. You can turn oranges into alcohol if you must, but unless you add sugar to the juice, you will not achieve more than a few degrees of alcoholic strength. Grapes are unique in the level of alcohol they can attain without additional sugar (though this does not stop many wine producers from, legally, adding it to increase alcohol).

A gift from God? Or an invitation from His fallen angel to become a minority alcoholic? We may, I think, creep away at this point and leave it to the theosophers to dispute these niceties.

A LITTLE HISTORY (NOT ALL BUNK)

Britons have never been healthier since they dumped beer and took up wine. Fifty years ago, barely four percent of us drank wine.

Now over seventy percent of the population drink it as part of their everyday lives.

It isn't only the UK that has been transformed from a beer nation into a wine one. Even in countries such as Thailand, whose king was advised by his doctors to drink a glass or two of red wine a day, there is interest in wine (and the country now has vineyards as well). Yet the health benefits of wine were known to the ancient Greeks, who believed, without knowing precisely why, that it had a role in strengthening the heart. Hippocrates, as long ago as 500BC, wrote that 'Wine is fit for man in a wonderful way, provided it is taken with good sense by the sick as well as the healthy.'

In America, even during the period made infamous by the passing of the most insane piece of social legislation ever drafted by a so-called civilized country – the Volstead Act, which led to Prohibition – it was still possible for angina sufferers to get phials of red wine from pharmacies upon presentation of a doctor's prescription.

A LITTLE MORE HISTORY (COMPLETE BUNK)

The Americans have carried the subject of wine and health to very entertaining lengths. A Kansas City newspaper, in an edition from 1900, ran a column expounding the virtues of French wine to the extent that it was claimed to be a universal panacea.

A daily glass of Médoc, so it was claimed, relieved 'allergic complaints'. Four glasses of dry Champagne were very good for 'liver weakness' and for 'coronary trouble'. Four glasses of Sancerre put paid to gout, and St-Emilion, also in a four-glass dose, tackled the menopause, would you believe.

The list of ailments that this Kansas City paper claimed wine will affect is startling. My favourites include the treatments for arteriosclerosis (three glasses of Muscadet and Provence rosé on alternative days) and for bronchitis (red burgundy heated to 140°F, with lemon peel added). There is, alas, no suggested wine for the boggled mind. Kansas City must have been a fun place to live in, to get seriously ill in, and doubtless to die in those barely-out-of-the-frontier years.

Nowadays, the list of medical problems wine can affect is also long, but there is more evidence for its efficacy. Let me begin by saying that I do not think you need telling that wine is good for you. But do you know exactly *why* this is so?

WHY WINE IS GOOD FOR YOU

And by 'you', I particularly mean *you*, madam. Although men derive huge benefits from wine (particularly to do with the heart), women and wine have a very special relationship.

Women have always had better memories than men (that's why they are better linguists). Wine, it now seems, can play a part in this. A recent US study found that women who drink alcohol in moderation may actually improve their memory skills. Women who had up to four drinks a day, it was reported, performed memory and mental tasks better than their teetotal compatriots.

However, the study also found that five or more drinks a day lowered mental performance in women. Interestingly, the research concluded that men who took five or more drinks a day performed the worst of all at completing the mental tests which comprised the study.

Wine *is* especially good for women, yet women have also been bequeathed a lousy deal, alcohol-wise, by omniscient Nature. Women do not absorb alcohol in the same way as men. As a result, they cannot tolerate it in the same way.

The precise medical reasons for this are wicked but irrefutable: women carry more fatty tissue per kilo of body weight than men, their bodies contain less water (so a woman's body fluids absorb alcohol in a more concentrated form), and, as if all that were not enough, due to differences in gastric activity between the sexes, a woman will, from the same glass of wine as a man, end up with more alcohol in her bloodstream.

Unjust? Maybe. But that's Nature for you. Take comfort from the fact that a woman has a superior ability to absorb languages and to decode the complexities of smells.

Now the good news. What cannot any longer be disputed is the healthiness of sensible wine-drinking by individuals (male and female) whose bodies can tolerate it. I have a pile of papers from university labs, medical centres, and research hospitals by my iMac as I write this and if I pull out one at random, what do I find?

That the healthiest wine is red and must also have been squeezed from especially fruity varieties of grapes such as Cabernet Sauvignon and Merlot, or any of several dozen other grape varieties. Red wine from any country can be healthy, but the more tannins in the wine (which I'll explain later), the better. Science, in the shape of chemists at Glasgow University, has not only confirmed this, but gone on to state that Chile is the country and Merlot and Cabernet Sauvignon are the grapes which, separately or together, create the healthiest wines you can drink.

Undertaken by a biochemical and life-science team led by a very unstuffy scientist known as Alan Crozier, what Glasgow University's research revealed was that the flavonols, the chemicals from the skins of red grapes, are highest in Chilean Cabernets and Merlots. It is these chemicals, or antioxidants, which combat the free radicals in the body that can lead to coronary heart disease (and are also implicated in other diseases such as cancer, Parkinson's, and Alzheimer's).

When I interviewed him years ago, Dr Crozier was quick to point out that it isn't only wine his team investigated. They discovered that, as far as flavonols are concerned, the cherry variety comes out top in the tomato league, as does the red onion over white in the onion stakes.

Chilean wine-growers couldn't believe their ears when they heard the revelations about their grapes. At last, it had been proven:

Chilean reds were not just full-blooded in flavour but full-blooded in scientific fact.

So just why *are* Chilean wines so well-favoured? It is because Chile's unique geographic location and climate means that the grapes hang longer on the vine and enjoy not only lavish hours of sunshine, but also cold, maritime-influenced nights, which lead to the development of the thicker skins, which, in turn, contain more of the beneficial chemicals.

However, later research from the Glasgow team also found that Bulgarian reds were brilliant as well, and that the French have sound claims for their wines (in particular those from Bordeaux and the Rhône). My own view is that red wines from any country work as well as the Chilean wines, although it is true that sunnier climes produce healthier wines.

All in all, it is now generally accepted that red wine from anywhere can be a 'health' drink.

WHAT'S MAGIC ABOUT RED WINE?

Red wines in general are reckoned to be good for human beings in many ways, and I am grateful to the Alcohol in Moderation organization (AIM), which promotes 'the responsible consumption of alcohol', for providing me with the current medical thinking on the subject.

Thus, it is not only coronary heart disease (thromboembolic stroke) against which wine can protect the drinker. There is now research to suggest that wine-drinking is associated with lower risks of dementia, has a beneficial effect on insulin metabolism, may have a beneficial effect on bone mass (staving off osteoporosis), and may also play a healthy role in estrogen replacement therapy (ERT).

The suggestion with ERT is, and I quote from an *AIM International Digest*, that 'moderate alcohol intake interacts significantly in a complex manner with ERT to modulate response to therapy'. I was also pleased to see scientists saying that 'alcohol taken moderately at mealtimes is unlikely to influence weight gain', as I have long scolded the fatheads who believe red wine is more fattening than white.

HOW DOES WINE HELP THE HEART?

It does so by encouraging the lowering of the wicked cholesterols (low-density lipoproteins, or LDLs) in the body. It does so by helping the development of saintly cholesterols (the high-density lipoproteins, or HDLs). It does so because it acts as an antioxidant and thus helps to prevent the wicked cholesterols from building up in the walls of blood vessels. It does so because it stops blood clots forming due to its anticoagulant activity. It also helps, as the Aussie doctor and wine producer Phil Norrie has written, 'by relaxing you and reducing stress, which is a contributing factor in vascular disease'.

From this (unscientific) observer's point of view, I am in no doubt that moderate wine-drinkers lead happier lives, and, as a psychological by-product of this, healthier ones. I believe that miserable people get ill, happy and positive ones are less prone; and wine plays a part in this.

There is now scientific evidence to lend credence to my belief that the body-changes caused by laughter play a role in disease and illness inhibition. To enjoy life is to be healthy. Or as the German aphorist Georg Christoph Lichtenberg put it: 'Moderation presupposes enjoyment. Abstemiousness does not.'

Well, I would agree with old Georg, wouldn't I? I spend half my life laughing and enjoying myself; the rest I spend drinking wine. Both expenditures, I believe, have long had a hugely beneficial effect on my health.

BEING A MERE MAN...

...not only excludes me from some of the curative properties that are claimed for wine, as discussed above, but also from one further extension: skin-care products aimed at women.

I often venture into recipes for dishes, health issues, the politics of wine-growing regions and so forth. But what on earth is the world coming to when I feel compelled, for exactly the same reasons as I might, say, write about the environmental implications of Portugal's cork industry, to talk about a range of women's skin-care products? The answer, as it always does, goes back to wine.

The news of these products was first brought to my attention a couple of years ago, when a reader sent me a report in the *Daily Mail*. The paper said that a model called Carla Bruni, doubtless famous to everyone but me, was a fan of these products, as was Princess Caroline of Monaco. The range was first sold in France in the middle 1990s.

This is hardly the type of news that would normally wrinkle my smooth indifference to matters of beauty, but the report said that this range of products, called Caudalie, was the brainchild of the woman whose château and vineyards in Bordeaux produce one of most rampantly fruity red wines in the region. It is called Château Smith-Haut-Lafitte, a wine for which I have a deal of affection.

Most enthralling about this aspect of wine and health is the nature of the chemical base of this skin-care range. It is made from the grape pips found in the *marc*, the pomace left over from the pressing of the grapes (skins, pips and so on). To make Caudalie, grape pips are specially purchased – so they are not, alas, the same as those that went into the tannic Smith-Haut-Lafitte.

But who cares? Not the rich folk who buy the stuff, obviously. Apparently, applications of Caudalie reduce wrinkles (how old is this Carla Bruni, then?).

Well, I'm no spring chicken and I don't think I'm especially alligator-skinned, and so anti-wrinkle cream is not a priority, but what is interesting is that my smooth condition (tolerate this small conceit) may be a result of thirty-five years of red-wine drinking, including many applications over the years of tannic reds – including Smith-Haut-Lafitte.

WHY DOES RED WINE MAKE FOR BETTER, AND
POSSIBLY MORE PRODUCTIVE, SEX?

Down in the boondocks of southern France,
in Minervois, there lives a very cheerful
chappie called Frank Chludinski. Frank, an
American chemist of Polish extraction,
seems to have stumbled upon a patch of
paradise. Anyway, he's married a local gal
and he makes wine there and jolly
invigorating stuff it is. Frank's Big Red is a
massively fruity concoction and it is on sale
at high-street chains in the UK.

On its back label, Frank's Big Red once
quoted a letter received by its maker from a
very grateful friend and customer. This fellow
revealed that, after drinking quantities of Big
Frank's Red, he successfully impregnated his
wife after many failed attempts. What the

back label does not say, but which Frank swears is true, is that the epistolic stud is a man of seventy and his wife some considerable years younger (five decades, I believe). I shall leave aside the interesting question of quite how many years this couple had been trying for parenthood and content myself with offering congratulations.

Now positive proof, you may think, is hard to come by to substantiate such as story as the one above. However, in April 2002, *The Guardian* newspaper covered a story about the published results of a Danish study of 30,000 mothers. According to the newspaper, 'A little alcohol each week seems to shorten the time women might take to become pregnant when they are trying for a baby...'

The study, which took three years to complete, was published in the journal *Human Reproduction*. According to Ms Mette Juhl, a member of the study team, 'We do not expect alcohol to improve a woman's fertility, but a moderate intake may correlate with a higher frequency of intercourse... small amounts of alcohol may have a positive impact on the female reproductive system, perhaps by helping women to feel relaxed.'

All this is good news. But there is some bad. According to a major global study, 'drinking a single glass of wine a day increases a woman's chances of developing breast cancer by around six percent'. However, in *The Guardian* of November 13, 2002, it was reported that one of the co-authors of the study, the epidemiologist Sir Richard Doll, said, 'We don't want to discourage people from having one or two drinks a day if they enjoy it.'

Well said, Sir Richard. And, if I may say so, a crucial qualification of the research, which is really nothing to get overly worked up about. An increase in the chance of developing breast cancer by six percent does not mean an increase by six percent for every drink enjoyed. If it did mean this, no woman would ever drink again (or could).

You have to consider that six percent in the light of the percentage chance of a woman developing breast cancer over her lifetime. This is one in nine. A six percent increase in that percentage figure is no reason to become teetotal.

2

why wine matters
to food

*In this short section, I am going to offer some
ideas on which wines go with which foods.
The perfect marriage is possible – and
certainly, it is always worth seeking out.*

Prosaically, wine will render harmless many of the bacteria associated with food, some of which may cause tummy upsets. In other words, wine is a benign killer. It aids digestion.

Most of us enjoy wine simply as a drink, and in this respect it has taken the place of beer in many people's so-called 'drinking repertoire'. However, wine and food together make a wonderful marriage, and it is one of the most neglected, and least appreciated, aspects of wine criticism. Hopefully, I can now make a few adjustments to this state of affairs.

Before I dive right in, however, let me make one thing clear. If you enjoy old red wine with blueberry cheesecake, or sweet white with your lamb stew, then no one can tell you that you're wrong. Taste is individual, and no one has precisely the same idea when it comes to food-and-wine matching.

May I start, then, by making the case for German wine with food?

THE CASE FOR GERMAN WINE WITH FOOD

I know, I know. I'm being deeply (and to some people, offensively) unfashionable. However, not only is fine, single-estate German Riesling the greatest white wine in the world, it is also one of the most sublime wines to have as a partner with so many of the different ethnic foods we enjoy today.

Good German Riesling is whistle-clean and subtle, with a beautiful texture to the fruit. It has texture and a touch of honey, and it is these which make it so valuable a partner to the spicy food of India, Thailand, China, Pakistan, Bangladesh, Japan, and Indonesia or indeed the so-called ethnic-fusion cooking of the trendier eateries.

Of course, some of the names of these wines do not exactly trip off the tongue. They are difficult to pronounce. But they are worth encountering. Best of all, prices make these wines a real steal, with some mature specimens going for less than or around a fiver.

THE CASE FOR ALSATIAN WINE WITH FOOD

Much of what I have said about German wine applies also to Alsatian wine. Wines from this incredibly dry and beautiful part of France work well with Oriental food, yet they also work with more European dishes.

Gewürztraminer

Try Gewürztraminer with certain cheeses. In Alsace, they always pair this wine with the local Münster, which, though delicate on the palate, is hell on the nose as it smells like the inside of a footballer's boot after a European Cup final. Bries and Camemberts, and certain goat cheeses, work wonderfully with Gewürztraminer.

Tokay-Pinot Gris

Try Tokay-Pinot Gris with rare game dishes where there is a sweet or sweetish sauce. Almost everyone thinks such food must have a red-wine accompaniment. But with a cherry sauce, cassis-based sauce or gravy, the apricot richness of the wine goes superbly with duck.

Riesling

Try Riesling with roast chicken. Alsatian Riesling is rather richer than the German variety, a touch raunchier and feistier.

Roast chicken and tarragon with such a wine, especially if it's a few years old, can be a sublime match.

Muscat

Try Muscat with scallops and other shellfish dishes. The spice of this wine and its flowery undertone are perfect with crustacea. One of the most perfect combinations is Muscat and scallops with a purée of peas and mint.

THE CASE FOR RED WINE WITH FISH

The white-wine-with-fish, red-wine-with-meat rule was, up until a few years ago, cast in iron, writ in stone, and had the blessings of convocations of gourmets. In the days when it was so immortalized, the rule was strictly observed. And the days we are talking about here are the days of Trollope and the invention of postage stamps, of Dickens, of the Crimean War, and right up until thirty years ago, more or less.

In the days before Chilean Merlot, Aussie Shiraz and Cape Pinotage, there was hock, Chablis, claret and burgundy. There was grilled sole. There was roast beef. These wines and those dishes had specific alliances that no one transgressed. It was right that rare roast beef went with claret, with all its tannins, because the blood in the meat reacted chemically with the tannins in the wine and one softened the other. Rare roast beef, or indeed any rare meat, can make a tannic wine more palatable. Likewise, the simplicity of grilled fish was suited to the white wines of Germany and France.

But nowadays we eat a much wider repertoire of dishes from all over the world. We eat spicier food. The most widely consumed dish in the UK is curry. Can any French or Spanish or Italian wine go with it? Well, a few. But much more willing to sit down with Oriental food are the wines of the New World. They were made (by accident – but it is a very happy accident) for these dishes. Thus, the old rules have gone out of the window.

I eat lots of fish and drinks lots of red wine. I often pair the two. Of course, smoked fish or shellfish are best with white wines – but even here there are no rules. I once drank *Jurassic Park* actor Sam Neill's home-grown Pinot Noir with his wife's dish of green-lipped mussels, and it was a delicious combination.

I find that dishes of cod, haddock, or monkfish with complex sauces go better with red wines. These wines can be anything from Sicilian reds to Barolos (which match sea bass perfectly) through to Aussie Shirazes and Californian Zinfandels. Loire reds made from the Cabernet Franc grape are, lightly chilled, superb with almost any fish but mackerel.

I first learned my lesson about throwing rules out of the window in 1972. I was sitting in the corner of a French restaurant waiting for my cassoulet and sipping (or should I say 'chewing'?) a glass poured from my bottle of Cahors, the red of the Dordogne made from grape juice so thickly clotted you'd swear you could grease an axle with it. An extremely ancient gentleman arrived and plonked himself at the table next to mine, barely a foot away. He was joined by an unsettlingly young and disturbingly gorgeous woman.

I tried to concentrate on my book, but how could I? The old man ordered his turbot and his companion's to be cooked rare so that 'the bones show up pink', and to go with this he told the sommelier to bring him a bottle of 1949 Château Pape-Clément.

I was thunderstruck. A red Graves, and a very old one at that, with a half-cooked turbot? Unbelievable. But do you know something? That old man and his young guest had the most marvellous time. They loved the food; they adored the wine; they laughed fit to burst at each other's *bon mots*. And here was I, a young Turk with his regulation cassoulet and dutiful Cahors, and I thought to myself, 'I am being taught a great lesson in how to live here and it would be a crime not to remember it.'

Now I cannot say that I relish the idea of old Bordeaux with grilled flatfish, but if it turns you on, go for it. There are no rules; there are only tastes and, as vividly as old men in restaurants, you can do as you see fit.

In South Africa I have often been offered Pinotage to drink with the grilled local seafood delicacies, and the combination works perfectly. Indeed, you can drink any young, fresh, fruity wine such as Pinotage from the Cape, Syrah from the Languedoc, Kékfrancos from Hungary, Blauer Zweigelt from Austria, Valpolicella Classico from

Italy, or Chinon or Bourgueil from the Loire, or Pinot Noir from Alsace with fish. Serve the wine lightly chilled, and the effects will be even better.

SOME PERFECT PARTNERSHIPS

Invariably, I am asked to match the wine to the wrong ingredient.

People say they are having lamb, for instance, but they neglect to add that it is stuffed with a spicy forcemeat and comes with saffron sauce. A mackerel will be the proffered bride to my wine, but in fact, the wine will have to marry with a mustard sauce. 'We're having prawns,' said a man to me once, forgetting to point out that they were to be marinated in a Thai dip and barbecued.

In other words: always consider the strongest ingredient in a dish – not just the biggest component of it. Here, then, are twelve additional approaches to creating the most successful wine-and-food marriages.

1 Chilean Cabernet with anything (except oysters)

2 Australian Shiraz with Indian food

3 Cava, the Spanish bubbly, with smoked salmon

4 Rioja with fish cakes

5 South African Pinotage with pasta covered in pesto sauce and bacon bits

6 Fino sherry and stir-fried prawns

7 Pinot Noir and roast chicken with tarragon and huge amounts of garlic

8 Chianti and mushroom risotto

9 Australian Semillon with Chicken Kiev

10 New Zealand Sauvignon Blanc with Thai fish and poultry dishes

11 Moscatel de Valencia with ice-cream (and with Greek yoghurt and honey)

12 Montilla, from Spain, with fish and chips

3

why wine rules
don't always matter

*Why corks aren't the only way to
seal wines. Why wine matters more than
experts. Why higher prices don't always mean
better wines. Why soil and climate are less
influential than you might think.*

As a wine writer, I would like my readers to taste the same wine that I have. I would like each wine to be as good as its maker intended. I want every wine to be exciting. The traditional cork seal prevents this.

WHY CORKS DON'T MATTER

Every wine is a blind date. Your author was born, so his mother often said, with beautiful blonde curls. Who would believe it now? The curls have disappeared over the years in various great and glorious causes, some too harrowing to be recounted in this book. Such losses are acceptable, I tell myself, if one is to participate to the full in life's frighteningly rich pageant.

However, what I do not find remotely acceptable is the forced uprooting of the last strands from my once angelically hirsute head by the failure of wine waiters to hand me a bottle of restaurant wine in decent enough condition to drink. I am, dear reader, often driven to tearing out my own blesséd hair. The catalogue of disappointments, near-misses, accidents, failures and down-right disasters is long and has seen all manner of absurd theatricals – from the chef storming out of his kitchen to remonstrate with me to the *maître d'* losing his temper and accusing his client of being so drunk he couldn't tell a hawk from a handsaw.

But what the restaurant trade knows full well, as do I, is that there is a wine assassin on the loose. He cunningly and subtly spoils a proportion of wines, possibly as much as ten percent. His methods are undetectable until the wine is in the glass (and not even then if you are in the presence of certain incompetent restaurant staff and wine-trade salesmen). This assassin's name is Duff Cork. He has a long and infamous history. You do not want him sitting down to dine with you – whether you are in a restaurant or have just bought a bottle for supper from your local supermarket.

Cork taint, for which the cork industry is desperately trying to find a cure, is caused by a rogue chemical called 2-4-6 Trichloronisole (TCA). It is created as a result of the chlorine cleansing the tree bark undergoes before it becomes a wine seal.

Richard Riddiford, the managing director of New Zealand wine producer Palliser Estate, once remarked to me: 'I know that I'll have 30,000 bottles of wine a year which have been affected by cork taint, 18,000 of them very obviously. We get less than twelve bottles a year returned in that time. Yet we have a clear policy of replacing corked bottles. So I deduce that people either don't notice the taint or, in many cases, don't like the wine and never buy our product again. What other luxury item in the world would put up with a guaranteed ten percent failure rate? We'll go over to screwcaps one hundred percent.'

However, tainted wine is only one of the problems cork confers on a wine. Since no single cork, however healthy and untainted it may be, is the same as the one lying next to it on the bottling line, each cork makes each bottle different. Sometimes the variations are wide, sometimes very small. But all corks, especially those inserted in wines designed to be cellared for a few years, cause variation among bottles. You truly do not know what you will get with a wine sealed with a cork until that cork is pulled.

So it is that supermarkets and New World wine producers are becoming united in doing something about eliminating cork taint and bottle variation by turning to alternative closures. Restaurants seem less willing to fight the good fight, though there are a few brave trendsetters out there who will instantly replace, without demur and even with a smile, any wine with which the customer finds fault. (There are even sommeliers who are in favour of screwcaps.)

I urge food guides to publish in their next

editions a list of restaurants pledged to treat customers in a civilized fashion when they find fault with a wine. Indeed, I would go further. I would recommend that guides refuse to list any restaurant where the finding of a fault with a wine is a hazardous business that may result in unpleasantries (thus food guides could immediately strike off Le Manoir aux Quat' Saisons in Oxford, where I was once subjected to a long session of torture when the management, including chef Raymond Blanc himself, refused not only to accept that a wine was faulty but to bring me a fresh bottle of it).

Is it any coincidence that, in the establishments where there is a problem with complaining about wine the sommeliers are male? Tush, that I should introduce the sexist idea that men are too arrogant to accept the idea that the wine they are offering to a customer might be at fault – which seems to imply that they are also substandard – but I do ask the question.

Women seem so much more willing to divorce the fault of the wine from any personal implication of incompetence. A little while back I went to lunch at 192, the notoriously fashionable eatery in London's Kensington Park Road, and I was forced to send back three glasses of different wines inside five minutes for being faulty. I had not ordered a whole bottle. I only wanted a glass with my lunch, and the restaurant, in which I have been eating since the day it first opened, has always offered a dozen wines by the glass. For the fourth glass I asked the extremely understanding wine waitress to open the bottle in front of me. She did so. I noticed she did not smell the cork.

So I carried out this routine maintenance check for her. The cork smelt of nothing but wine. The wine was, then, perfect. Why did you not, I enquired, smell the cork to ascertain if there might be any taint? She replied that in her wine-tasting lessons she received from the Wine & Spirit Education Trust, the lecturer told her this was not necessary.

I corrected her and demonstrated exactly why it is imperative to smell the cork. Why? Because a cork is supposed to be a purely neutral seal. Thus it should smell only of wine. If it does so, then the wine is perfect and requires no further olfactory investigation.

If the cork smells musty or cardboardy or mushroomy, then it may – and I emphasize *may* here – have contaminated the wine.

We are now at the root of the problem. Cures for cork taint have been proclaimed by the cork industry, it is true, but they seem only to affect a fraction of the million of corks produced each year, and the jury is very much out on their effectiveness. The problem, if we continue to use natural cork, will not go away. The problem will only be completely solved if we use plastic corks or, better still, screwcaps.

I am happy to report that supermarkets have now all recognized the problem with natural cork and are turning to a plastic which looks and performs like cork but IT DOES NOT TAINT THE WINE. (Though it is also true that plastic corks are not as pliable as natural corks and can sometimes be stubborn and difficult to remove and cannot be reinserted into the bottle without effort.)

Now I'm not going to claim that each and every plastic-corked wine will knock your socks off, but I can claim that none will be riddled with TCA. I can also claim that in each and every case the wine will be, barring the odd storage mishap, closer to the condition its maker would prefer. I can also claim that you have no need to smell the cork to ascertain if the wine is in good condition.

I am a very happy wine writer knowing that the wine I will drink, and will describe to you, will be more like the wine you will discover in the bottle if natural cork is not present. It will not be another version of the wine.

For wines that are designed to be drunk immediately and not cellared, plastic corks are fine. I do not recommend such wines for laying down. The latest research suggests that plastic corks can cause air to enter the bottle over time.

Why not test one or several of the widely available plastic-corked wines next time you have a dinner party? Hand the corkscrew to the nearest available man (a wine buff will do perfectly), and say, 'Alphonse, will you do the honours?' And so Alphonse, unsuspecting guinea pig, will twirl that spiral of steel in his fingers, insert the point, and puff and pant on your behalf. But will he remark on what he finds at the end of that corkscrew? Probably not. He will be fully taken with his triumph of entry and successful extraction.

Thus he may never notice that the cork is plastic whatsoever. Few people do. The makers of the things are not only careful to ensure the material is taint-free and made of a food-approved polymer but coloured so cunningly that a nesting bald-headed eagle might mistake it for cork.

But cork it is not. Spoil the wine it cannot. Spoil the party it cannot. Of course, screwcaps would be even better, but this means you cannot hand over the corkscrew any more. Screwcaps, as I said earlier, are even better than plastic corks, as many Australian and New Zealand white-wine producers have discovered. With the screwcap, you get to the wine with a simple twist of the top and the wine stays fresher (though it will still mature in the bottle).

Does a screwcap kill the romance of the wine? Not if the fruit in the bottle is sexy. For, surely, doesn't the romance of wine lie in the liquid in the glass, and not in the maintenance of old-fashioned rituals like corkscrews?

Well, the plastic cork does keep the corkscrew in business. But tomorrow, in the next ten years, I predict more and more wines will be sealed with screwcaps, thus making even plastic corks old-fashioned. Mark my words: one day the corkscrew will be consigned to the dustbin of history.

Indeed, I believe that the plastic cork is a stage on the road to the screwcapping of all wines one day. Pigs will fly, you say? Perhaps. A screwcap guarantees that the wine is always in the condition its maker wants it to be. Both red and white wines benefit from aging without any air getting in or wine fumes out, and as more and more retailers introduce screwcaps, these facts are becoming understood and appreciated. It costs more to screwcap a wine than to cork it. But isn't wine worth it?

It is a scandal that, in this third millennium, we have a product sold worldwide which is so uneven in performance. No other edible or drinkable item is made with such a hit-or-miss attitude. Would beer- drinkers tolerate a failure rate of one can in ten? And their favourite tipples being different from one pub to the next? Would soft-drink fans cheerfully tolerate similar failure rates and variations in taste? The answer is no – and a very resounding no. But because wine has been portrayed as a special liquid, full of ritual and tradition, too many drinkers accept these problems as part of the price they have to pay to participate.

You do not have to pay it. It is a lie. It is a lie maintained by snobs and wicked wine merchants and self-serving wine writers.

It is time we cried: 'Enough!'

WHY WINE MATTERS MORE THAN EXPERTS

People who say they are experts always defend their expertise. I would like you to develop a healthy scepticism of experts where wine is concerned.

Don't believe the frauds who tell you wine is a difficult subject that only a few gifted individuals know anything about. The everyday drinker knows something about wine about which the so-called wine buff or wine critic has not the remotest inkling. And that is: what YOU like to drink.

Critics are a self-obsessed species. Their absorption in their subject is often what stands in the way of them actually enjoying it like a normal human being. I have enjoyed glorious evenings in the theatre, at the cinema, and in restaurants, all of which were damned by the critics; it's the same with wines. I have my own preferences for certain wines, but equally I do not find it irksome or difficult to put myself in the place of a readership that may have a partiality for wines of an utterly different temper. This requires an act of the imagination of a different order than the creativity required of a writer.

I can't drink any wine without considering what it represents as an object of value for money (or not), and this, as far as I am concerned, is what legitimizes what I do. I taste with my readers' pockets in mind (this does not mean cheap; it means that the bottle is worth every penny).

The artificial nature of the formal wine-tasting mitigates against these kinds of judgements. The number of wine critics who can consistently produce useful judgements about wines and how they will perform with food I can count on the fingers of one hand.

I am entirely of the opinion that the huge reputation of many New World wines in this country is due almost exclusively to wine writers assessing them favourably in wine-tastings when in fact many of the wines, were they to be considered in partnership with food, would have to be rated as altogether different artefacts.

Add to this a widespread inability to provide value-for-money judgements and you have what in other professional circles would be regarded as a professional crisis – but then, wine writing is not a profession (beyond almost all but a few writers on wine).

The individual wine writer is valuable only in as far as you can judge that his or her palate matches your own, and therefore he or she is likely to feel the same way as you might about the same wines. The wine writer worth his or her salt is a wine enthusiast.

In the winter edition of the 1936 *Wine & Food* magazine, the old poet Hilaire Belloc remarked: 'I have found in my own life two rules with regard to wine… The first is: go by your palate; and the second is: Go by the results.' To which I would add, 'Go *buy* the results, too.'

Trust your judgement. Exercise your palate. It is yours. It is unique. Remember Oscar Wilde's advice: 'Nothing worth knowing can ever be taught.'

Few times in my wine-drinking life have I encountered bottles that might have justified their legendary reputations (but never their vast outlay). These were a 1947 Château Margaux drunk in 1966, which was aromatically wondrous, and a Château Lafite 1934 drunk in 1984, which, though slightly austere (still!) from the tannin overlapping the fruit, did go brilliantly with a whole Bressé chicken roasted with forty cloves of garlic.

WHY PRICE DOESN'T MATTER

Don't listen to the old lie that says you are *always* better off paying £9.99 for a bottle of wine than £3.99.

Traditional wine merchants have had their backs against the wall. In their attempts to fight the supermarkets and high-street wine chains (but more especially the former) which have so many wines costing between three and four pounds, they often peddle a little fairy-tale. This tale would have you believe that spending more of your money on a bottle of wine is better value because more of the money, due to the horrendously high duty on wine in the UK, goes to maker and not to the exchequer.

Do not listen to this drivel from the wine establishment and their lubricious lackeys

why wine rules don't always matter   75

(*i.e.* stuffy wine writers) about the virtues of the higher-priced bottle. They are blathering through their bruised backsides.

WHAT ABOUT DUTY ON WINE?

Every bottle of wine, whatever its final retail price, whether £2.99 or £15.99, has to pay well over £1 in duty. This is a fixed rate, but the amount of the final sales tax which is added, via VAT, is variable, and so this also increases the financial burden on the final purchaser. However, clearly in a cheaper bottle of wine, a greater proportion of the final purchase price goes in duty than with a more expensive bottle.

All this is true. Yet what it ignores, utterly and cynically, is economies of scale. A wine producer once said to me, when I asked him if his French wine co-op liked selling his wines so cheaply to UK supermarkets, that he loved it. 'You know, Malcolm,' he said, 'if I sell my wine for £5 to 200 different wine merchants in your country, I will make less money than if I sell it for half that to just one supermarket. Why? Two hundred invoices are a lot of trouble, and I can wait a long time for some people to pay me. With one sale of say, 100,000 bottles, I get paid within sixty days, always, and my money is working for me faster and I can reinvest it faster. There is no contest in my opinion.'

This is why so many supermarket bottles of £2.99 and £3.99 wine are so tremendously good. Everyone involved in the deal is making a healthy return because the turnover is so high. The merchants' argument for higher prices has, then, no substance because it offers no guarantee of a better wine on the basis of the greater return available to the producer.

Of course, the proportion of profit of each single bottle sold of the cheaper wine is less than with a more expensive bottle, but the producer is not concerned with individual bottles; it is the total sold that is the meaningful statistic. A producer can make more money in the long run and have a healthier business if he sells wines more cheaply.

WHY SOIL AND CLIMATE MATTER LESS THAN YOU MIGHT THINK

The French possess a genius for marketing the products of their agricultural labours. The word *terroir*, a French term which has no precise equivalent in English, is used internationally to refer to the unique siting of a vineyard and its soil and climate. Think about it: if you made something which began life from the fruit of a plant, would you not wish to suggest that it is where that plant grows which makes the fruit unique?

This is *terroir*. Or course. It is unique. The plants are grown only in that patch of soil. This is certainly *terroir*, but it does not confer any further status. Yet we live in a world where provenance, and the perceptions that result and are encouraged to result from this, count for more than the reality of the taste and smell and performance. Be utterly sceptical in these circumstances. Trust your taste.

In ham we have Parma, with salmon we have Scotland, with chocolate we have

Switzerland, for example. Is each the best there is? Nonsense. The Spanish *jamón de serrano* is the equal of Parma's any day; New Zealand salmon is richer and more deeply flavourful than any Scots fish; and the French themselves produce better chocolate than the Swiss. I could list many more examples, but you get my point.

The idea that a uniquely sited patch of soil will make a wine equally unique and so worth a fortune is complete rubbish. It is *how the wine is made* that is important.

The New Zealander Professor Warren Moran, who makes a study of the subject, put it to me that vines define the essence of the place where they are grown only taking into account the human factors; if the factors change, then so does the *terroir* (and thus the wine). To consider, then, *terroir* as an immutable phenomenon is absurd. Yet this fairy-story underpins the whole French concept of the *appellation contrôlée* system. It is naïve, added Professor Moran, to associate *terroir* simply with soil as many textbooks tend to do.

WHAT, THEN, IS THE GREATEST INFLUENCE ON WINE? The mind and hands of the man or woman who makes it. The soul of the winemaker is a greater factor in the quality of a wine than the soil of the vineyard.

Must we be such such slaves to our prejudices when it comes to matters of appetite? It seems so. Many drinkers, though they like wine, love status symbols more. They are prejudiced in favour of wine they have heard is grand. They choose such wine over lesser-reputed wines and so lose out.

Also, many drinkers actually lack the olfactory faculties to deeply appreciate the nuances of wine (usually men; women are much more sensitive to the minutiae of smells and tastes). In these cases, spending a lot of money on a wine is part of the sensual thrill of drinking it. What must it be like to open and consume a bottle of wine which costs thousands of pounds? Incredibly, on the palate it may be no different from opening and consuming a bottle which costs a fiver. But think of the impact on the pocket! This is not a book of sexual theory, but I cannot help but point out that for many a male drinker, putting his hand in his pocket and digging deep provides the real thrill of the liquid in the glass.

Fostered by wine writers and critics, wine salespersons and publicists, and especially upmarket wine merchants, expensive wines maintain a hold on the imagination. I do not say that some of these wines are not magical, that some are not superb, but I do say that all are overhyped and very, very few are worth the money.

'I think spending £15 on a bottle with a name like Pommard on the label,' said a bloke to me once in Tesco, 'means I'm going to be trying out a terrific glass of wine.' No amount of cajoling from me, even to the extent of offering to buy him a £3 bottle of Romanian Pinot Noir to compare (and probably find tastier), would change his mind. No woman, I maintain, would ever be so wooden-headed.

4

why the wine world
must change

*My, how the world has moved on!
(And why it is useful for you
to know this.)*

Ten years back, I visited a Bordeaux vineyard to interview a young Australian woman who had recently been appointed winemaker there. The vineyard had been newly acquired by a Norwegian violinist – very progressive. I asked her how the locals had taken to the idea of a woman in charge of making the wine.

'No problem,' she said. 'The two-hour lunches take getting used to, though, and…'

'Yes?'

'Well, when I first arrived, people looked at me strangely, and I thought, "That's because I am a stranger and I'm not French." And then they asked me, "You are the winemaker, aren't you?" And I would say, "Yes, that's what I do." And they would say, "But you're from Australia. Do they have vines in Australia?"'

It is now safe to say that the natives of that

particular part of Bordeaux, and indeed all Bordeaux, and Burgundy, and the Rhône and Champagne, and pretty much everywhere they produce wine in France, now realize that, yes, they do indeed have vines in Australia. The legendary parochiality of the average French wine-man and -woman has been shaken, and Australia is the cause. Australia has made spectacular inroads into the most important and prestigious export market the French have, the so-called United Kingdom, and it seems that nothing can stop it.

When I became a wine writer in 1988, I would estimate that the French share of the UK wine market was around thirty-seven percent. The Aussie share was around 1.5 percent or less. Today, the Aussie share is over twenty percent. The French share, which has been declining for the past decade, is down to a little less than twenty-four percent.

This is an astonishing set of statistics which, in spite of Disraeli's dictum ('There are lies, damn lies, and statistics'), are the visible proofs of some wonderfully damned truths: 'French' wine is in trouble, is rent with dissent, hampered by archaic wine laws, and its famous wine regions are kept going only by snobbery and tradition.

How has this state of affairs come about? Firstly, it is important to understand that there is no such thing as merely French wine. Hence my use of the quotation marks above. France is a patchwork of many wine regions, and they have to be treated separately, particularly with regard to making a distinction between *appellation contrôlée* areas (designated vineyard areas, often known as AC) and those under the freer laws of *vin de pays*, or 'country wine'.

I would certainly not condemn all wines from the old-established regions such as Bordeaux or Burgundy, where AC laws, though often broken, condemn growers to approved grape varieties and written-in-stone methods of viticulture. Yet the genuine value-for-money great wines in these places are few and far between, and the Aussies have them beaten on both fruit and price.

The Rhône is more exciting, as are the Languedoc and Roussillon, and so we cannot simply blanket all French wine as suffering from the same, dead hand of a long and glorious past. However, even with the Rhône's Syrah, it is the Aussie version of the same grape, Shiraz, that is preferred by many drinkers for its greater softness and sweetness.

So are we Brits losing our taste for certain French wines? And if so, why? Because – and this is the nub of the Aussie's success – we have in the UK a new wine market, a new wine buyer, and new wine thirst.

When I was born, less than four percent of this nation drank wine. That figure is now more like seventy-four percent. This market is not yet wholly mature; it is young, it is fuelled by a desire for sweet fruit and relaxed tannins in reds, and a rich melon quality in whites, neither of which is found in the general run of French wines – certainly not the traditional ones.

The British appetite has also changed. Indian food is the most popular in the land, and we also eat lots of other ethnic foods. French wines do not go with these cuisines. But, by a delicious coincidence, rich Chardonnays and soft, sweet-edged Shirazes go perfectly. In other words, what has happened in the UK wine market is nothing more or less than the old story of a complacent and outmoded product being challenged by a feistier newcomer more suited to changing tastes. It has happened in motorcars, vacuum cleaners, haberdashery, computers... The list is long.

For me, it is an exciting time to be writing about wine. It is a time of challenge and opportunity. The French, as always, will rise to both, and the vast investments in vines in areas such as Burgundy and Bordeaux mean that these regions will not be allowed to wither and be replaced by Disney theme parks or small wine museums catering to label-spotters. I prophesy that Burgundy will, within half a century, become once again the exemplar of all that is great in Pinot Noir and Chardonnay, and Merlot and Cabernet Sauvignon in Bordeaux will develop to cater for changing tastes.

But the French change slowly in these matters, and it takes a crisis to shake them. Remember: they have a strictly taught historical system which gives them an arrogance and a sense of their regional uniqueness that is utterly foreign to us Brits. It is much stronger than, say, the accented mind-set that differentiates a Cornish person from a Scot or a Cockney, even though, on the surface, there appears a world of difference.

WHY APPELLATION CONTRÔLÉE IS A JOKE

People often ask me if the words *appellation contrôlée,* under the wine name on a bottle of wine, are a guarantee of something. Yes, they are: of bullshit. They're a guarantee that you're going to be buying a fairy story. Many drinkers of French wines imagine that those legendary French words convey a guarantee of excellence, but nothing could be further from the truth. *Appellation contrôlée* simply means a controlled name.

Every time I enter a wine shop, or poke about a branch of a high-street wine retailer, and even when I nose about a supermarket's wine shelves, I always come across the odd customer, sometimes whole groups of misguided folk, flying in the face of reason and buying a bottle or bottles of wine purely on the basis of their belief that the words on the label that refer to a vineyard area or a region represent some kind of seal of approval. Yet *appellation contrôlée* is a self-serving system that has nothing to do with quality. Let me present the following horror story, which illustrates why, for some people, everything is in a name.

In early 2002, Richard Riddiford, managing director of New Zealand wine producer Palliser Estate, had me riveted with a fascinating account of one of his trips abroad.

'I was in Taiwan a short time ago,' he said, 'showing retailers my wines. A businessman takes me out to dinner. He asks me: "Do you like Château Pétrus?" I say, "Well, yes; wouldn't anyone?" He says "Okay," and orders a bottle of the 1982 vintage – and a bottle of Coca-Cola. Don't ask me how many thousands of Kiwi dollars the Pétrus must have cost. He pours me a glass. It's wonderful. Into his glass of Pétrus he pours some of the Coke. I stare in disbelief. I ask, "What's with the Coke?" He says, "I don't like the taste of the wine by itself." And he turns the bottle round so the label can be seen by diners at other tables.'

What is Château Pétrus? It is one of Bordeaux's most famous reds. The '82 is a legendary vintage. It goes for thousands of pounds at auction. In April 2002, at Christies of South Kensington, for instance, six bottles of Château Pétrus 1990 were sold for £4,510. I'm sure they'll sit very nicely with Coke; just as the appearance of the wine at that Taiwanese businessman's table sat very nicely with his reputation for luxury and connoisseurship.

In a similar spirit of status-symbolism, men all over the world are cellaring wine in the same orgy of acquisitiveness as they garage vintage Bentleys and hang old Picassos. Such men may never drink, rarely drive, or ever give their Pablos a second glance, yet they have created one of the silliest snobberies connected with wine.

Wine is simply the fermented liquid of grapes. It can be sensuous beyond belief. It can be rough as old shoe leather. Both are acceptable interpretations and have their place. Showing off with expensive bottles and wine-collecting for the same motives have nothing to do with wine. They have much more to do with the insecurities of the collectors, the greed of the sellers, and shallowness of the belief that status is dependent upon luxury objects.

5

which wine names matter & why

*What matters on a wine label.
The truth about vintages.
Some suggested producers,
broken down by country.*

So, if words such as *appellation contrôlée* can mean so little, what *does* matters on the label? Obviously, in a book such as this, I cannot recommend individual wines and vintages. However, I can offer some guidelines, and throw in some ideas that will help you find where the best – that is, the 'best-value' – wines can be found.

Firstly, let me offer you this. Supermarket own-label wines in the UK can be marvellous. Do not turn your nose up at them (as snobs will). The idea that own-label means horribly cheap, and relatively cheerless, remains (surprisingly) a widespread delusion. It goes back to the days when supermarkets did not employ the skilled professional wine-buyers that they do now. In the old days, they merely bought any old filth, and thus, in that faraway age when men thought a trolley was something that bought the drinks around, own-label wines were basic, crude, and nowhere near as well-made as they are today. Supermarkets were also non-interventionist in those days. They didn't work hand in hand with producers and vineyards to fashion wines to suit British palates; they simply bought the cheapest stuff they could, off the shelf.

Today's own-label wines are usually single grapes or blends – of two grape varieties and also, sometimes, two different vintages. But the level of consistency I have observed in these wines over the past three years has impressed upon me that their policing by retail buyers has ensured a very high level of consistency year on year.

Wines today are of greater technical stability and cleanliness than ever before. And this statement applies to the cheapest bottle of own-label supermarket wine. The professional buyers of such wines now work closely with the winemakers on the ground. This is the key to consistency and good value, and, oft times, real excitement for little financial outlay.

To be fair, not all of these wines are outstanding; some are merely drinkable, others are just cheerful plonk. Yet there are also certain own-labels, widely available, that are just plain terrific. I refer to the own-label red and white Chilean, South African, Australian, Southern French, Spanish and Italian (often Sicilian) wines that dominate the own-label ranges. These wines can flirt with highly flavoured food, for they exhibit the depth of fruit needed to accompany dinner-party roasts and grills without wilting.

When I have a large gathering around for lunch or dinner, I invariably pour half-a-dozen of such reds into two large jugs (three bottles in each), and thus tedious wine chat is kept to a minimum. All you hear is 'Oooh, can I have a another glass please?' or 'May I help myself?'

Wine is a social lubricant without equal. It does not have to give rise to pretentious blathering, except between bores.

EVERY GENERALIZATION IS A SIN...

... which is a generalization. One of the great abiding myths is that of the vintage year of a wine, or of the region it comes from. 'Oh the '59 Bordeaux!' merchants will coo. Or the '82. Or the 2002.

This blanket assertion that somehow the magic of climatic conditions (sunshine with a fancy moniker) confers its blessing on a whole region or country is utterly absurd. It is a lie.

Of course, it is true that during a certain growing or picking season an area might have enjoyed terrific weather (or the reverse), and this will have affected the vines and their fruit. But to say that this means that all the wines made in that area are therefore wonderful (or the reverse) is to ignore the human factor.

Grapes cannot ripen without sun, yet these same grapes cannot be pressed into wine without technology and its manipulation by winemakers. These winemakers vary in temperament, skill, outlook, ambition, luck and genius. A wine is different every year due to Nature, and it is different every year because of Humankind.

Why do I tell you this? Because I am about to add to this lottery. Not by naming vintages, but by identifying wines whose names I think you should remember and consider worthy when you are shopping. I am going to generalize.

People often ask me what I buy to drink when I go to France or Spain or Italy on holiday. Is it always the wine of the region? Interestingly, the answer is, 'No'. I approach wine the same way wherever I am in the world: I judge it on taste.

Once, on holiday in Provence with a local giant supermarket only three miles away carrying a huge selection of wines, I discovered that the best local drinkable wine was not Bandol, Côtes du Provence, Lubéron or even the Rhône. It was a Chinon, grown several hundred miles north in the Loire. The supermarket had it for around fifteen francs a bottle (call it £1.50). No comparable wine grown locally was under forty francs.

I bought a single bottle of the Chinon, opened it and tasted it in the car park, went back inside and bought three dozen bottles to keep our little party in everyday red for two weeks. To be sure, I also went around some of the local châteaux and co-ops and bought a few interesting, more expensive bottles. But it was the Chinon everyone remarked on and enjoyed, whether it was served chilled or at room temperature.

I did no more and no less than any intelligent person would have done: I shopped with my head screwed on. My head, admittedly, is full of names like Chinon, Chianti Rufina or Toro Tinto, but the process is simple. I saw the name on the shelf and saved a fortune.

May I help you towards a similar discipline? The following are the wine names to look for on supermarket shelves. I have broken them down into countries. In each, I offer areas of interest and, where I can, specific names of producers or vineyards.

ARGENTINA

The red and white wines of the region of Mendoza can claim to be among the most exciting on UK wine shelves. The grape varieties to look for are Bonarda, Cabernet Sauvignon, Chardonnay, Merlot, Sangiovese, Sauvignon Blanc, Shiraz, Tempranillo, Zinfandel, Viognier – and also various blends of these.

The names of the best producers' wines are Adiseno, Alamos, Anubis, Argento, Bianchi, Bright Brothers, Candela, Catena, Corazon, Etchart, Fabre Montmayou, Familia Zuccardi Q, Graffigna, J&F Lurton, Magdalena River, La Nature (organic), Norton, Picajuan Peak, Río Santos, Santa Julia, Terrazas, Trivento, Valentin, Villa Atuel, Viña Amalia, and Weinert.

WHY THEY MATTER

The unusual level of tannic richness in Argentina's reds and silky svelteness in its whites make the wines stand out. Prices are almost always reasonable, reflecting great credit on their makers' patience and passion. The latter seems most evident in the wines, which appear warm, smooth, deeply human and hugely engaging. Argentinian wines represent potency with elegance, style with humour, depth with delicacy. Only the country's economic problems and a lack of business sophistication stop it from becoming a larger exporter than Chile to the UK. Argentina matters because it has the exciting potential to become one of the world's most significant wine nations.

Australia

Regionally, I am greatly fond of Shiraz from McLaren Vale, Riesling from the Clare Valley, Cabernets and Chardonnays from Mount Barker and Margaret River in Western Australia, Chardonnay from the Hunter Valley, also the Cabernet, Riesling and Chardonnay from Coonawarra... and I could go on and on. And on.

All-Aussie names to look out for include Tim Adams, Alkoomi, Annie's Lane, Bailey's, Bannockburn, Barramundi, Basedow, Bass Phillip (rare Pinot Noir), Bethany, Bleasdale, Brokenwood, Brown Brothers (especially the late-harvest Muscat), Grant Burge, Campbells of Rutherglen (Muscat), Cape Mentelle, Capel Vale, Chain of Ponds, Chapel Hill, Chateau Reynella, Chateau

Tahbilk, Clancy's, Coriole, Cranswick, Garry Crittenden, Cullen, D'Arenberg, Dalwhinnie, Deakin, Delatite, Devil's Lair, Dromana Estate, Andrew Garrett, Giaconda, Grossett, BRL Hardy (including Hardy's Coonwarra Cabernet and E&E Black Pepper Shiraz), Heggies Vineyard, Hill-Smith Estate, Hollick, Honey Tree (an M&S label), Houghton, Howard Park, Jasper Hill, Jindalee Estate, Kangarilla Road, Katnook, Killawarra, Knappstein, Leasingham, Leeuwin, Estate, Lenswood, Lindemans, Maglieri, Mamre Brook, Geoff Merrill, Michelton, Mildara, Morris (sweet whites), Moss Wood, Mount Helen, Mount Horrocks, Mount Ida, Mount Langi Ghiran, Mountadam, Nepenthe, Normans, Nottage

Hill, Oxford Landing, Padthaway Estate, Penfolds Bin 28 Kalimna Shiraz, Penfolds Bin 128 Coonawarra Cabernet, Penfolds Koonunga Hill, Penley Estate, Petaluma, Peter Lehmann, Pewsey Vale, Pirramimma, Rockford, Rymill, St Hallett, Saltram, Seppelt Great Western, Shaw & Smith, T'Gallant, Tatachilla, Temple Bruer, Vasse Felix, Wakefield, Wendouree, Wirra Wirra, Woolpunda, Woolshed, David Wynn, Wynns Coonawarra, Yalumba (especially the Merlot, Shiraz, Viognier), Yellow Tail, and finally, Yellowglen.

WHY THEY MATTER

No longer is there such a thing as Australian wine. Like France and Italy and Germany, Australia is a land of many regions with varying characteristics that are evident in the wines' textures, flavours and suitability for various foods. This has made Australia matter more than ever.

Australian Shiraz may seem like a generic brand, and in a way it is, but it expresses itself very differently in Mudgee from the Hunter Valley, McLaren Vale from Barossa, Margaret River from Coonawarra, and the Clare Valley from Orange. This added complexity in the wine map of this incredible – and incredibly large – island means that there is added complexity in the wines, and drinkers (trained ones) are beginning to appreciate the differences in regional variations, just as they do between a wine from the Rhône and one from Bordeaux.

Australian wine matters so much because it suits such a wide range of foods as well. Since Australia has become an Asian power, or rather is becoming one (for there is still a reluctance in some quarters to give up afternoon tea and roast beef on Sundays), the nation has become altogether more important and exciting.

The influx of so many different nationalities over the past twenty years, each with its own ethnic cuisines, has meant that Australia has developed a fantastic food style of its own: one based on a very high level of quality raw materials from vegetables and fruits to fish and meat. By a wonderful coincidence, Australian wines, red and white (and indeed sparkling), go better with this sort of ethnic-fusion cooking than most mainstream European wines.

This is why Australian wines matter more with a Thai green curry or a tandoori chicken. This is why they matter so much to the new generation of wine-drinkers and healthy eaters.

AUSTRIA

Not much seen in supermarkets, the odd Lenz Moser Blauer Zweigelt apart (a fleshy red sassier than many Beaujolais). However, Austria is Europe's best-kept wine secret. The locals guzzle their wines with enthusiasm – which is the main reason that so little is exported. The whites are made mostly from a grape called Grüner Veltliner, but Riesling and Pinot Blanc are also grown.

If you see these names, then open your wallet: Aigner, Feiler-Artinger, Freie Weingärtner Wachau, Heinz Hirtzberger, Franz Hopler, Jurtschitsch/Sonnhof, Moosbrugger (Schloss Gobelsburg), Munzenrieder, Willi Opitz, and Pfaffl. These are the ones I know best. There are hundreds of other good producers. Count your blessings if you come across one.

WHY THEY MATTER

Austrian wines and producers matter because they represent one of the great outposts of individualism in Europe. The grape varieties are their own, the producers have huge, committed ideas of quality and quirkiness, and with varieties such as Grüner Veltliner (white), they can create wines to rival Riesling. Now and then, a producer of St-Laurent (a red variety) turns out a wine to rival a great red burgundy. Nor surprisingly, Austrians, being smart people, drink most of these stunning wines themselves.

BULGARIA

Domaine Boyar is the most well–known name, but Cabernet Sauvignons and Merlots, as well as local varieties such as Gamza, are to be found under own-label names, and they are excellent (for the most part). Bulgaria, as Thrace, supplied the Greek troops in the Trojan War, and those guys had a thirst.

WHY THEY MATTER

Bulgaria has not had a smooth ride since the demise of the old socialist regime (which, with its subsidies, helped the wine industry turn out a uniformly fruity and value-for-money product going back thirty years). Since the freeing up of the economy, the wine industry has struggled, but major producers like Domaine Boyar have borrowed from the European Bank and invested heavily in new facilities. It matters that the Bulgaria vineyards continue to thrive and turn out inexpensive but high-quality Cabernets, Merlots and Gamzas.

CHILE

This benign-climated vineland has become a huge success with famous varieties of grapes. It is difficult to find a poor Chilean wine (though some are less than good). The big four varieties are grown in abundance: Cabernet Sauvignon, Merlot, Chardonnay and Sauvignon Blanc, but Pinot Noir and Gewürztraminer are also starting to appear. Many are simply stunning.

Chile's most reliable names include the following: 35 South, Antares, Caballo Loco, Caliterra, José Cánepa, Casa del Bosque, Casa Doñoso, Casa Lapostolle (especially the Cuvée Alexandre designation), Casa Leona, Casablanca, Concha y Toro, Cono Sur, Dallas-Conte, Errázuriz, Gato Negra, Isla Negra, La Palmería, Las Colinas, Las Lomas, Luis Felipe Edwards, Mont Gras, Montes Quiltro (label for Oddbins), San Pedro, Santa Inés, Sierra Los Andes (M&S), Terra Mater, Trio, Valdivieso, Veramonte, Villa Morande, Viña Carmen, Viña Gracia, Viña La Rosa, Viña Porta, Viña Santa Carolina, Viña Santa Rita, and Vistasur.

CHILE... *continued*

WHY THEY MATTER

The sheer elegance of Chilean wine, red and white, is a benchmark for quality at a reasonable price everywhere in the world. The climate, the soil, the vineyards, the growers, the winemakers – the passion and committment are high and the wines have finesse yet with a power that can often take the breath away. It matters that Chile continues to be a beacon of style and richness. Without these producers, there would be a huge gap in our lives and on our shelves.

ENGLAND

Chapel Down, Shawsgate and Three Choirs have all made wines I have liked. There are 300 vineyards in England and Wales, but most are making simple crude whites for passing tourists.

WHY IT MATTERS

It doesn't, greatly, except as an adjunct to the tourist trade. A few vineyards aside, there isn't much point in raving about English winemakers or English wines. However, these vineyards matter, if only because they are part of our cultural heritage.

FRANCE

This country is so vast as a wine-growing region that offering individual names is impossible. Instead, I'd like to offer regions I think yield the best fruit for the easiest money. Let us, then, forget Champagne, Burgundy and Bordeaux and concentrate on the less glamorous areas.

For sparkling wines, look for Crémant d'Alsace and Crémant de Bourgogne.

For rich reds, go for wines from these villages in the Rhône: Cairanne, Lirac, Rasteau, Sablet, Séguret, Vacqueyras, Valréas, Vinsobres, and Visan.

For lighter reds, look for Bourgueil and Chinon from the Loire. These wonderful wines, made from the Cabernet Franc grape, are delicious chilled. Loire whites, Vouvray in particular, are also fine in both sweet and dry styles. The wines of the Languedoc are also interesting, as the quality has risen, the grape varieties have widened, and the supermarkets have been able to negotiate great prices for them.

There are, it is true, a bewildering number of names and thousands of producers in France, but regional appellations worth looking for are the following *vin de pays* ('country wine') areas: Vin de Pays d'Oc, VdP Catalan, VdP Pyrénees-Orientales, VdP de l'Aude, VdP de la Cité de Carcassonne, VdP des Côtes de Lezignan, VdP du Val d'Orbieu, VdP de l'Hérault, VdP des Coteaux de Murviel, Vdp des Coteaux du Libron, and VdP du Gard.

France... *continued*

Why they matter

France is the mother and father of the world's grape and wine industries, although the Romans introduced the vines (and the Greek introduced the idea to the Romans). These producers matter because they are so diverse, so political, so important, so cultural, so diverse, so local, so vocal, so heavily into their own expression of their own *terroir* (which is often a fiction, but they believe it). Without France, the world of wine would be as badly off as the World Cup without Brazil, Germany, Italy and England combined.

For many people, in spite of the inroads made into French wines sales in the UK by New World producers, France is the world of wine in one single country. It has set standards (then broken them). It has made rules (and then flouted them). It can make sublime wines from several dozen varieties. It can produce mediocre status symbols requiring a sackful of money to acquire. Everyone wants to beat France and to *be* France. France is the model that other wine countries try to follow. It matters that French producers have responded positively and creatively to these challenges because this activity enriches all our lives.

Germany

Ah, poor Germany: how its fortunes have fallen! Once, it yielded the Victorians' most expensive and highly rated white wines; now we new Elizabethans regard it mostly as sweet junk. However, marvellous wines are made from Riesling in the Rhine, Mosel and other areas. Personally, I think these are the greatest white wines in the world.

The following are the names to look for: JB Becker, Georg Breuer, Dr Bürklin-Wolf, Christoffel-Berres, Donnhof, Dr Fischer, Egon Müller zu Scharzhof, Graf Edelmann, Louis Guntrum, Fritz Haag, Heinz Wagner, Heyl zu Herrnsheim, Koehler-Ruprecht, Laurentiushof, Lingenfelder, Dr Loosen, Max Ferd. Richter, Maximin Grünhaus, Mönchhof, Müller-Catoir, Paulinshof, JJ

Prüm, Reichsrat von Buhl, Balthasar Ress, Schlossgut Diel, Dr H Thanisch, Villa Wolf, and Von Kesselstatt.

WHY THEY MATTER

Germans are infuriatingly precise about the way they classify their wines, but they are scrupulous at creating the greatest white wine on the planet from the world's finest white-wine grape: Riesling. There is, with the wines fashioned from this grape, a breadth of civilized acidity, complex yet immensely subtle, combined with a delicacy yet incisiveness of fruit that is incomparable.

Of course, several other important grapes are grown in Germany, but Riesling matters most. Here, this grape reaches its apogee of maturity, expressiveness and finesse. Germany *is* Riesling. It is among Germany's most impressive claims to possess and nurture civilized ideas. The German wine producers matter hugely to the world of wine because they are without equal. For the purest expression of a grape, it is to Germany that the drinker must, sooner or later, turn.

GREECE

The best wines in Greece come from Santorini and Macedonia.

WHY THEY MATTER

Greek wine regions, producers, and wines (don't underestimate Retsina; it can be exciting with food), are among the most important historical characters in wine. There is much interesting and varied wine made in this noble land from grape varieties never heard of by most of us. Greek producers matter because, perhaps more when one is in the country than when standing in front of a UK wine shelf, those whites and reds are rustic, characterful, honest and simply terrific with the local food. That food-and-wine combination is a unique language. It cannot, and will not, be lost.

HUNGARY

At present, the two outstanding exporters of Hungarian wines are Hilltop Neszmély and Ede Tiffán.

WHY THEY MATTER

Many people don't realize that some of the most colourful local winemakers live in Hungary. Most of their wines never see the light of day in a British wine retailer's shop, but Merlot, Chardonnay, Cabernet Sauvignon and Sauvignon Blanc (not to mention Gewürztraminer) are made there, and many represent great value and faithful grape varietal character.

Also, don't overlook Hungary's great sweet wine: Tokaji, or, in English, Tokay. This raisiny, marmaladey, uniquely fruity wine is a superb partner for foie gras, sometimes blue cheese and, occasionally, pastry desserts. It is a very special contribution to the world of wine.

ITALY

Of course, the wines of Barolo are wonderful, some of them, and the greatest are made by Angelo Gaja. The Valpolicella Classicos of various producers are also brilliant. The Amarones of this region can be total magic. The wines of Zenato, also from northern Italy, are never tedious, often exciting.

In Chianti, I always look for those labelled Chianti Rufina: less pretentious than *classico*, often showing more thrilling, herby richness. I love the white wine of Naples, Fiano di Avellino; the wines of Puglia (made from the Primitivo grape).

Sicily is building a class of wines that is all its own. The name of the great producer Planeta stands out here, but even a supermarket Sicilian red can be terrific.

Inycon is an excellent Sicilian wine covering half-a-dozen varieties of grapes.

Why they matter

Italy is unique in the world of wine, for it is the only country where every single region has its own grapes and its dishes that work with the wines those grapes produce. No other set of producers is out to marry its products with food so passionately. It is the *raison d'être* of such growers' lives. It is what they live for and crush grapes for: to create liquids that work sublimely well with all the local dishes.

As a result, Italian wines are uniquely food-oriented. It is even true that the newer, sweeter, brasher styles of wines from Apulia

(Puglia) and Sicily in the deep south are able to handle many of the ethnic-fusion dishes with which French wines are uncomfortable.

Italy is also historically important. Known as *Enotria* (the land of the vine) to the ancient Greeks, who first established colonies there and planted grapes, the Romans took on this mantle of vine-spreading, and as a result, we have a Europe-wide wine industry. Without Italy, there would be no world of wine as we know it, and there would certainly not be, with that element out of the equation, the New World wine phenomenon that we have and relish so much.

It was Italian immigrants to those New World lands who brought with them the love of growing vines and making wines.

Wherever an Italian makes his home, he thinks about producing wine. Wine flows in Italians' bloodstreams.

Mexico

LA Cetto is the one name to look for in Cabernets and Petite Sirah.

Why they matter

To give California the uncomfortable feeling that it isn't the only place in the region that can make wine. LA Cetto's vineyards are located in Baja California, and though this might be considered a blip on the wine map of the world (and not of much interest to many Mexicans, who prefer beer and Tequila), I like this blip and I like its wines.

Morocco

Rustic reds from here can be terrific. Don't look down your nose at anything with Morocco on the label, but investigate further.

Why they matter

North Africa is a superb place to grow grapes. Morocco's reds can be rich and very forward, but they are superb with Middle Eastern, Indian and other Oriental foods. And they are cheap.

New Zealand

The most reliable name across the board is also the country's second-largest producer: Villa Maria. It doesn't seem to matter what colour (red or white) or what grape – Sauvignon Blanc, Riesling or Merlot – Villa Maria turns out a beautifully tailored product. Montana's Church Road label is also brilliant with reds, while Montana's Marlborough Sauvignon Blancs, Rieslings and Chardonnays can be excellent.

However, when compared to major wine-producing countries, there is not a lot of choice when it comes to producers. New Zealand is a boutique wine producer and, statistically speaking, produces very few bottles of wine when compared with other countries.

That said, the great names to look for on any bottle of Kiwi wine are: Allan Scott, Ata Rangi, Brancott Estate, CJ Pask, Cairnbrae, Chard Farm, Cloudy Bay (including the sparkling Pelorus label), Coopers Creek, Corbans, Craggy Range, Delegat's, Esk Valley, Felton Road, Fromm, Gibbston Valley, Goldwater, Grove Mill, Hans Herzog, Highfield Estate, Huai, Hunters, Jackson Estate, Johanneshof, Lawson's Dry Hills, Matua Valley, Millton, Montana (the Church Road label and the Marlborough Chardonnay, Riesling, and Sauvignon Blanc), Morton Estate, Neudorf, Ngatarawa, Palliser, Rippon, Sacred Hill, Seresin, Stoneleigh, Te Mata, Vavasour, Vidal Estate, Villa Maria, and Wither Hills.

New Zealand... *continued*

Why They Matter

Because this is the land where wine has helped the Kiwis change from sports-obsessed royalists with one eye on Europe to a Pacific presence of great interest and topological fascination. Who wants to grow sheep and apples, when on the same land an exciting, international, sexy, profitable and healthy product like wine can be created instead?

In 1986, New Zealand stunned the world of wine when a single bottle of Cloudy Bay Sauvignon Blanc, when tasted alongside the then exemplars of this grape variety, Sancerre and Pouilly-Fumé from the Loire, was clearly noted to be superior. Since then, New Zealand has *become* Sauvignon Blanc (although it grows other exciting varieties, including excellent Chardonnay, Pinot Gris, and Merlot). I am less keen on the Pinot Noirs, unless grown for sparkling wine.

New Zealand and its producers are important and matter so much because they have put a bomb under Europe's wine producers and proved that a small set of islands can make world-class wines in small quantities, yet have a global impact. In 2002, New Zealand crushed just 120,000 tonnes of grapes. This is about as much as a large South African co-op might crush in a year. The same holds true for one of the big southern French co-ops. The Kiwis may well run a boutique, but like many such operations, its influence is greatly in excess of its output.

PORTUGAL

One region stands out for me, and its all red wines: the Ribatejo.

WHY THEY MATTER

Of course, Portugal has more regions than this one. There is also the Douro from which we get port: for me, the world's greatest fortified wine. Portugal and its history, its producers and its grapes matter because they have preserved a timeless sense of the colonial influence that is found nowhere else in wine. Many port companies are run by Brits who send their children to British public schools but who are bilingual and dual-nationals. These quaint people with their old-fashioned ideas are like a rare tribe on the edge of civilization it is necessary to preserve.

ROMANIA

Try the Pinot Noirs and Merlots. All are startlingly cheap, but now and then sheer silken brilliance emerges from the bottle.

WHY THEY MATTER

Romania is so-called because the Romans regarded it as an important province. So Romania has a history. It also has some excellent vineyards, and only economic factors have prevented the country from making greater strides in wine and exporting more. It matters to European unity and peace that countries such as Romania have thriving wine industries for local pride, work, wealth and individuality. That latter expresson, on a wide scale, is some decades away, but the potential is huge.

SOUTH AFRICA

South Africa produces frisky Cabernets, firm Chardonnays, and aromatic Chenin Blancs. It also boasts the unique Pinotage red grape, with its hot and spicy fruit.

Producer names to look for are L'Avenir, Avontuur, Backsberg, Clos Malverne, De Wetshof (Danie de Wet, Diemersdal, Delheim, Drostdy Hof, Neil Ellis, Fairview, Graham Beck, Hamilton Russell, Jeff Grier, Jordan, Kanonkop, Landskroon, Meerlust, Neethlingshof, Rust-en-Vrede, Simonsig, Thelema, Vergelegen, Villiera, and finally, Warwick Estate.

WHY THEY MATTER

Because it produces a different slant on the usual international varieties, because of that sexy Pinotage grape, and because the Cape wine industry can be one of the dynamic engines of change which will, one day, help turn the country into a modern economic success story and a model for multi-racial harmony and tolerance.

SPAIN

The only European wine nation able to climb in the ring with the New World fighters and get in a telling punch. Where Germany, France and Italy report falling exports to the UK in the face of wines from Australia, South Africa, New Zealand, California and South America, the Spaniards, in spite of a falling home market, go from discrete strength to strength. Why? Because where the French are arrogant and presumptive, the Germans technical and leaden, and the Italian off-hand and lazy, the Spaniards (in particular the Catalans) are dynamic, creative and also immensely hardworking.

The regions to take note of on labels are: Bierzo, Calatayud, Campo de Borja, Cariñena, Conca de Barberà, Condado de

Huelva, Costers del Segre, Jumilla, Navarra, Penedès, Priorato, Ribera del Duero, Ribeira Sacra, Rioja, Rueda, Somontano, Tarragona, Toro, Utiel-Requena, and Valdepeñas.

Great producers are Albet i Noya, René Barbier, Capçanes, Castillo de Montjardín, Julián Chivite, Conde de Caralt, Fariña, Guelbenzu, Jean León, Juvé y Camps, Marqués de Grigñon, Marqués de Monistrol, Josep Masachs, Masía Bach, Muga, Ochoa, Alvaro Palacio, Palacio de la Vega, Pesquera, Puig Roca, Raïmat (cava), Sarría, Jaume Serra, Scala Dei, Miguel Torres, Vilamartín, and Virxe dos Remedios.

Spain's other great vinous contribution to culture is cava, the sparkling wine. There are tremendous examples of own-labels cavas at supermarkets, some of them better than Champagnes at three times the price. Moscatel de Valencia, a honied white with an overtone of marmalade, is also brilliant with ice-cream and other desserts. All the supermarkets have own-label bottles, under £4.

Also, do not ignore sherry. It has become labelled, and indeed libelled, as the old fart's tipple, but fino and mazanilla make wonderful aperitifs, and palo cortado is a simply uplifting drink to welcome home the weary from work.

WHY THEY MATTER

Spain is Europe's most creatively dynamic country. It became so after November 1975 (when I lived there), when the Franco era passed and regions that had been stifled became newly energized and dynamic. Spain has wonderful diversity and local character, not only in music, film, design, books and food, but in wine. Is there a wine like sherry in the world? Quite like, yes, but nowhere near as exciting and potent. Is there a wine like Rioja? Only in other regions of Spain. Are there wines like Priorato from Tarragona, cava from (mostly) Catalonia, whites like Albariño grown in Spain's wettest and most Atlantic province, Galicia? No, no, and no (though Champagne, from whom the Catalans stole the recipe for bubbly, would protest – perhaps because cava now outsells Champagne everywhere). The world's most planted grape variety, Airén, is credited to Spanish vineyards.

USA

California is the number-one state here, of course. Everybody knows about California wines. The other two notable states, also Pacific-rimmed, are Oregon and Washington. Californian Cabernets, Zinfandels and Chardonnays can be tremendous.

The names I have found personally satisfying are Acacia, Atlas Peak, Au Bon Climat, Beringer, Bonny Doon, Byron, Buena Vista, Calera, Caymus, Chateau St Jean, Clos du Bois, Clos du Val, Dalle Valle, De Loach, Deer Park, Dry Creek, Duxoup, Edmeades, Kendall-Jackson, Far Niente, Fetzer, Foppiano, Franciscan, Frey, Frog's Leap, Gallo Sonoma, Geyser Peak, Grgich Hills, Groth, Iron Horse, Jekel, La Crema, J Lohr, Lucas, Lytton Springs, Matanzas

Creek, Miramar Torres, Robert Mondavi (the Coastal Series, though ignore the absurd Opus One from Mondavi/Rothschild), Mount Eden, Mount Veeder, Nalle, Joseph Phelps, Quady (dessert wines), Qupé, Kent Rasmussen, Ravenswood, Ridge, Saintsbury, Santa Cruz Mountain, Sebastiani, Shafer, Simi, Sonoma Creek, Stag's Leap, Unti, Villa Mount Eden, and Wente.

In **Oregon** I've found satisfaction in bottles carrying these names: Amity, Bethel Heights, The Eyrie Vineyards, King Estate, Kramer, Ponzi, Rex Hill, Serendipity, and Willamette Valley.

In **Washington State**: Columbia Crest, Château Ste-Michelle, The Hogue Cellars, Preston, and Staton Hills.

USA... *continued*

WHY THEY MATTER

It is not only with the Pacific-edged states that America has claim to interesting vineyards. There are others in several other states which grow vines, but it is undoubtedly to California, Oregon and Washington that this vast land owes its viticultural heritage.

And this heritage is not only historically important, but of great modern relevance. The sheer quality of Cabernets, Merlots and Zinfandels, Chardonnays and other white-graped wines that are produced in the Pacfic states has made America a world leader in wine. Not only is the world's largest wine factory in California, courtesy of Gallo, but this state has one of the world's greatest wine universities, the University of California at Davis, which is responsible for turning out graduates as well as new ideas in viticulture and oenology.

Without a vital and dynamic wine industry in the United States, the world of wine would be much less exciting and diverse.

a final word about enjoyment

In ending, let me just say this. The list of names in the preceding chapter is no more a reliable guide to beauty than my personal address list. Would you get on famously with all of my friends? Or even one of them?

Which is another way of saying that wine is a deeply personal thing. More than this, it is not a uniform product. Not only is each bottle different from every other bottle because of the differing circumstances in which they are drunk, but we ourselves change. A wine that appears delicious one day may not seem sublime the next. Add to this the lottery of the cork, so that changes make one bottle of the same wine different from its supposed brother, and you have a set of conditions with which no other critic in any other field has to contend.

I hope this book has been entertaining and enlightening. But it is just one man's view, one man's set of experiences, one man's set of prejudices and passions.

Bear this in mind as you form your own individual palate and develop your own outlook on wine. Above all, enjoy yourself. What else should wine be about?

Index